OREGON TRAIL

Troll Associates

OREGON TRAIL

by Laurence Santrey

Illustrated by Francis Livingston

Troll Associates

Library of Congress Cataloging in Publication Data

Santrey, Laurence.
   Oregon Trail.

   Summary: Describes the difficulties encountered by
settlers who traveled westward in covered wagons or
prairie schooners along the Oregon Trail during the
1830's and 1840's.
   1. Oregon Trail—Juvenile literature.   2. Overland
journeys to the Pacific—Juvenile literature.   [1. Oregon
Trail.   2. Overland journeys to the Pacific.   3. West
(U.S.)—History.   4. Frontier and pioneer life]
I. Livingston, Francis, ill.   II. Title.
F880.S23   1984   978'.02   84-2643
ISBN 0-8167-0196-2 (lib. bdg.)
ISBN 0-8167-0197-0 (pbk.)

The United States was only a few years old when the first American trail-breakers crossed the untracked continent to the far Pacific. Two of these daring explorers were Meriwether Lewis and William Clark.

Lewis and Clark brought back word of rugged, snow-capped mountain ranges, of rushing rivers, and of clear mountain streams. They described deserts and forests, abundant wildlife, and fertile fields. The picture Lewis and Clark drew of this magnificent area excited the imaginations of their fellow Americans.

Others added their accounts to those of Lewis and Clark. The mountain men, who ventured alone or in small bands into the wilderness, also brought back exciting stories. They told of huge herds of animals roaming the plains, and of both friendly and hostile Indians. They also brought back valuable fur pelts of beaver and otter and hides of buffalo and deer.

More and more settlers were moving west —out of the thirteen original states and through the Appalachian Mountains. Land was cheap and opportunity was unlimited. People believed that anyone willing to work hard could make a successful life "out West."

Settlers were encouraged to go west for many different reasons. The government wanted the western lands to belong to the United States. The best way to do this was to populate the West with Americans.

Eastern manufacturers wanted new markets for their products, and land agents wanted to sell pieces of their large land holdings.

The West presented a wide range of opportunities. It drew religious groups, such as the Mormons, who were seeking a place to live and worship freely. It drew missionaries, such as Narcissa and Marcus Whitman, who hoped to teach Christianity to the Indians.

Politicians and soldiers, such as Senator Thomas Hart Benton and Captain John Fremont, built careers and fame on the development of the American West. And people of all kinds—farmers and miners, merchants and traders, shopkeepers and craftsmen, adventurers and thieves, artists and scholars—hoped to find something good for themselves out there.

By the 1830s, the land between the Atlantic Ocean and the Mississippi River was well settled. The time was ripe for the great move to the Far West.

And in the next fifteen years many families from the East left their farms and city homes to join the trek. It started in Independence, Missouri, the jumping-off place for the wagon trains that would travel the 2,000 miles to the Oregon territory.

The first step in preparing for the long trip was to sell everything that couldn't fit into a wagon and wasn't absolutely necessary. Settlers took along farm tools, axes, guns, food, clothing, the family Bible, and just a few prized possessions.

Sometimes, people tried to take along some lovely old piece of furniture or other family treasure, only to discard it along the way. Each year, settlers would see things along the trail, abandoned by those who had passed that way the year before.

An overloaded wagon wore out the oxen pulling it and slowed the progress of the whole wagon train. Any delay in their progress could mean disaster and death, as many settlers learned.

In order to complete the five- to six-month journey to Oregon before winter closed in on them, the wagon parties had to leave Independence in the early spring. Independence, Missouri was a bustling town on the Missouri River.

One of its best-known features was Smallwood Nolan's inn, the westernmost hotel in America. It wasn't a very elegant hotel, but it could hold four hundred guests—as long as they were willing to sleep two to a bed.

The town itself was mostly tents and covered wagons, with just a few buildings. The buildings were blacksmith shops, stables, and stores where travelers stocked up on provisions for the trip ahead.

Independence was also where the wagon trains were formed. A wagon train usually had from twenty to one hundred families, each with its own wagon, oxen, horses, and dairy cow. Sometimes, a number of families formed a wagon train before they reached Independence. Other wagon trains were made up of families that met in Independence.

Most of the families that traveled the Oregon Trail in the 1840s were respectable, middle-class people. The trip wasn't possible for a poor family. It cost between $700 and $1,500 to assemble a wagon, animals, and the gear required for the journey. That was a lot of money in those days. The only way for a poor person to make the journey was to "hire on" as a driver or servant.

Before they left Independence, the families elected a wagon-train leader and a number of other officers. Then they agreed on rules and regulations to be followed on the trail.

Fights and friction between families were part of the long, exhausting trip. So it was wise for the wagon train to prepare for trouble by having rules and a form of self-government.

Most wagon trains hired a scout, or pilot, to lead the group across the country. The scouts were mountain men or former soldiers who had been over the terrain many times before.

They knew which trails to take, when to stop and when to move on, where it was safe to go and where it wasn't. Wagon trains that followed the advice of their pilots usually made it to Oregon in good shape.

The first part of the Oregon Trail, across the prairies and alongside the Platte River, was easy going. The trail was wide, the animals and the people were fresh, and the wagons were in good condition.

These wagons were called prairie schooners because their canvas covers reminded people of the sails of a ship. Except where the trail passed through narrow valleys, the prairie schooners moved along in columns of two or four. That way, they could be grouped together quickly, to defend against attacking Indians. At night, the wagons were parked in a large square or circle, and the animals were driven inside this wall of wagons.

As long as a wagon train stayed together, kept its animals from wandering off, and didn't stop for too long, the threat of an Indian attack was not great. If a wagon dropped behind the train and was traveling alone, the danger of being attacked by Indians increased. Most of the time, however, the wagon trains had only peaceful contact with Indians.

Most of the travelers on the Oregon Trail never saw any Indians except friendly ones. These Indians lived in and around the forts that dotted the trail.

There were five main forts used as stopping places between Independence and the end of the trail. They were Fort Kearny, Fort Laramie, Fort Bridger, Fort Hall, and Fort Boise. These installations were like little walled cities in the middle of nowhere.

Inside the fort was a big, open, square area surrounded by storerooms, offices, and shops for merchants and trappers, and cabins for soldiers. The corners of a fort's walls had two-story blockhouses, with slits for rifles.

Indians often camped outside a fort's walls. They would stay there for months to trade with passing wagon trains and with the people who lived in the fort. Some Indians also worked in the fort, or hired out there as scouts.

Between Fort Laramie and Fort Bridger the wagon trains crossed the Rocky Mountains. A highlight of the trip was when they reached South Pass and crossed the Great Divide.

On the eastern side of the Great Divide, the rivers ran down the mountains toward the Atlantic Ocean. On the western side, the rivers ran toward the Pacific Ocean.

Reaching the Great Divide was a welcome boost to everyone's spirits, since the push up into the Rockies was rough and expensive in terms of lost wagons and animals. The trail down was even worse, with everyone struggling to keep the wagons from hurtling down the steep mountainsides.

Once past the Rockies, the problem was water—or the lack of it. Now the Oregon Trail took the train through the dry, high plains of Idaho. Even where there was water, it wasn't always drinkable. Many oxen died after swallowing water from the poisonous alkali springs.

But relief came to the wagon trains after the final push through the Blue Mountains. It brought the weary travelers down into the green valleys of Oregon. There, along the Columbia River, was fresh water and good grazing for the animals.

Even after the settlers reached Oregon, there was still a lot of work to be done. They had to find good farm land, clear it, build on it, and work the land. But the worst was behind them. And the experience of the trail had toughened them.

The great migration along the Oregon Trail brought thousands of people west. They were followed by the forty-niners, rushing to California for gold.

But the day of the wagon train was ending. The railroads and the telegraph were changing the face of the West. Eventually, wind, weather, and civilization wiped away almost all trace of the Oregon Trail. But nothing can ever erase the effect it had on the building of the American West.